D1794816

EMPOWERED

EMPOWERED

Original Inspirational Quotes
For Life, Love and Laughter

ANDREA CAMPBELL

Pocket Learner Publishing

ISBN: 978-1-914997-00-6 (sc)   978-1-914997-33-4 (hc)

To the memory of my grandmother – Mrs. Iris Ingram Steele, who inspired me to live my life in the pursuit of excellence, with gratitude, and in the service of others.

I want to dedicate this book also to families everywhere who care for disabled children and adults, in their endeavor to provide inspiration and boost aspirations.

A GIFT FOR YOU

Please join our mailing list to receive periodic updates and materials. You'll also be able to keep abreast of our future publications.

As a thank you, please visit the following page or scan the QR code to download a set of original inspirational posters that you can print, frame and position in your favorite space.

http://eepurl.com/h8SU31

TABLE OF CONTENTS

INTRODUCTION

This book, "EMPOWERED", is the result of divine inspiration and life lessons. The 120 quotes are part of a broader set of quotes compiled over several years. I published this book because I felt that these life truths came not "from" me but rather "through" me, and it is my distinct honor to share them with the world.

They inspire critical thinking at varying levels and boost social cohesion, allowing everyone to participate, irrespective of their academic, social or economic status. People interpret them in various ways, and they are best appreciated when shared in group settings, whether in the classroom, the boardroom, places of worship or among families and friends. Once explored, they are open to varying interpretations and lessons are often learnt in the process.

I hope those who explore these quotes find them soul-searching and enjoyable. I hope they will be inspired and energized by them as they seek to make sense of life.

As someone who works with people, helping them to identify where they are and where they want to go, I have applied these quotes to inspire and empower many as they build their personal and professional lives. The quotes are a powerful medium for change, and I have benefitted from them, being the parent of a child with special educational needs.

When Shari was born and I learned of her condition, I couldn't see any light or reason to hope. I felt powerless and alone, and it took a long time for the darkness to go and the light to appear. I am a better person for the experience, and my life has a new focus – I now help parents to inspire and empower their children who struggle to learn. I would never have embraced that mission had my daughter not been born. I would never have written this book or my other books, and I would not have developed the innovative multi-award-winning Pocket Learner system – an Educational Development program that exists to promote learning in children with special needs.

Parents, caregivers, and educational practitioners alike use the system to promote reading, vocabulary building, and counting in children with learning difficulties. When I look at this experience, I consider the quote: "In the darkness, you can't perceive of the light; then the light appears, and suddenly, the darkness has purpose." I have expanded on this quote later in this chapter.

The quotes are best appreciated when each is explored individually. Readers are encouraged to peruse them individually and allocate time for self-exploration. Consider what the statement means and how it applies (or not) to your life. Think about people, places, and things and consider how your life and that of others could improve based on the message implied in the quote. They are good starting points for idea generation and to flesh out issues that may be hidden. They are meant to prompt questions that are often not asked, the answers to which are not usually considered. I have outlined below some examples of how this might be presented.

Quote 1: "In the darkness, you can't perceive of the light; then the light appears and suddenly, the darkness has purpose."

Interpretation: Life has dark moments, but once you experience them, you realize they have value.

Considerations:
- What have you gone through in life that has challenged you?
- What have you learnt from the process?
- How has the situation changed your outlook on life?
- Has the experience improved your life?
- What do you have to be grateful for, and to whom?
- What could have happened had you not had that period of darkness?
- Darkness is ignorance, and light is knowledge – what are you ignorant of?
- How can you increase your knowledge in that particular area?
- What light can you bring to someone else and the wider society?
- What relationships have you lost, and how have you handled the break?
- What relationships have you gained, and how have these improved your life?
- How have you empowered yourself after a major loss?
- What struggles have you endured, and how have you overcome them?
- Have you used your experiences to empower anyone, and how have these helped your healing process?
- Do you track the healing process and watch the growth?
- Have you discovered why all of it had to happen?

- How has your life improved after the period of darkness?
- Whom have you inspired consequent on your access to light?
- Have you become more spiritual, and what does spirituality mean to you?
- Do you have hope?
- Whom can you use your experience to help?
- Are there opportunities coming from this experience?
- Can you establish a business out of your opportunity?
- Has your experience been life-changing?
- Whom can you use your experience to serve, and how?
- How have your goals changed since your experience?
- What have you learned about yourself in the process?
- What advice can you offer to others going through the experience?
- How often do you remind them that they are light and should shine?

Quote 2: "It is better to run with winners and lose than to run with losers and win."

Interpretation: Don't measure your achievements against those who are weaker than you.

Considerations:
- Who are the people in your circles, and what can you learn from them?
- Who is your mentor, and whom are you mentoring?
- Are your relationships empowering you or hindering you?
- Do you have baggage that you need to drop?
- What is your measure of success?
- Is this a realistic measure?
- Whom do you admire and why?
- Are you a good role model?
- Who are your competitors, and what are they doing better than you?

- Have you learned the pattern of their growth and why they stand out?
- Are you the best in your industry, and what do you need to grow?
- Do you need to acquire new "friends" (personal and professional)?
- From whom can you learn?
- Do you have access to someone who can help you?
- Who's in your ecosystem?
- Who's setting the trend in your field?
- Who are the winners/influencers in your field, and what are their characteristics?
- Are you empowering losers or are they pulling you down to their level?
- How are you being influenced?
- What do you need to learn in order to improve/enhance your position?
- Where can you get the knowledge from?
- Do you believe you deserve or can do better?
- Are you afraid of failure?
- What risks have you taken, or are you willing to take?
- What skills do you have, and what are the skills gaps?
- What tools do you need in order to compete effectively with others?
- Are you pursuing your dream or someone else'?
- What does winning look like, and what does it mean to you?
- What do you do when you fail? Do you try again or give up?

Quote 3: "You can never soar like an eagle if you sustain the mind of a chicken."

Interpretation: All change starts in the mind; empowering your mind is the start of a successful life.

Considerations:
- What is your greatest fear?
- What is stopping you from progressing?
- How do you spend your time?
- Who are those in whom you invest your time?

- What preoccupies your mind?
- Do you have specific, measurable, achievable, relevant and timed (SMART) goals?
- Are you an introvert or an extrovert?
- Are you more confident on your own or in a group?
- What is your attitude to risk?
- Are you growing?
- Do you have the courage to speak in public?
- What do you need to learn in order to get to the next level?
- Are you confident enough to approach people you consider more powerful than you?
- How do you handle influence (either good or bad) from people?
- Are you being hampered by past events in your life?
- Can you challenge your fears and change your mindset?
- What are the barriers to a change in mindset?
- How do you nurture your mental as well as your spiritual health?
- Do you have the appropriate life/work balance?
- What literature are you reading/programmes are you watching?
- Have your found your purpose in life, and are you pursuing it?
- Are you ambitious enough?
- Do you have the right resources to fulfil those ambitions?
- Does your purpose align with those around you?
- Are you aiming high enough?
- Are you satisfied with your life?
- What baggage do you need to drop?
- Do you want it bad enough?
- Are you surrounded by mediocrity?
- What tools do you need?

PART 1

LIFE

Blessed are those who find wisdom, those who gain understanding for she is more profitable than silver and yields better returns than gold.

Proverbs 3: 13-14

A cocoon protects you but also limits you;
emulate the butterfly and break out!

A "Fact" is a statement of truth; your opinion doesn't change it.

A pig is happy
when left to
wallow in mud;
it needs no
analysis.

A pig placed in a stable does not become a horse; it will still grunt!

A poverty mindset
is not inherited;
it is cultivated!

A spade is a
spade,
sometimes we
have to call it
as it is!

A small dog grows up and becomes a big dog.

A tree that grows
in a rubbish
dump does not
produce
rubbish.

At some point in
our lives we have
to be willing to
risk being
somebody's fool.

At some point
in your life you
have to let go of
your baby.

Big things are made up of small things; embrace the small things.

Birds have flight
built in
fish have swim
built in
you've got a gift
built in
it's up to you to
find it.

Burying and
planting
are similar
processes
but oh how
different is the
outcome!

Don't be upset
when people
stop listening
if you are
singing the
same song all
the time.

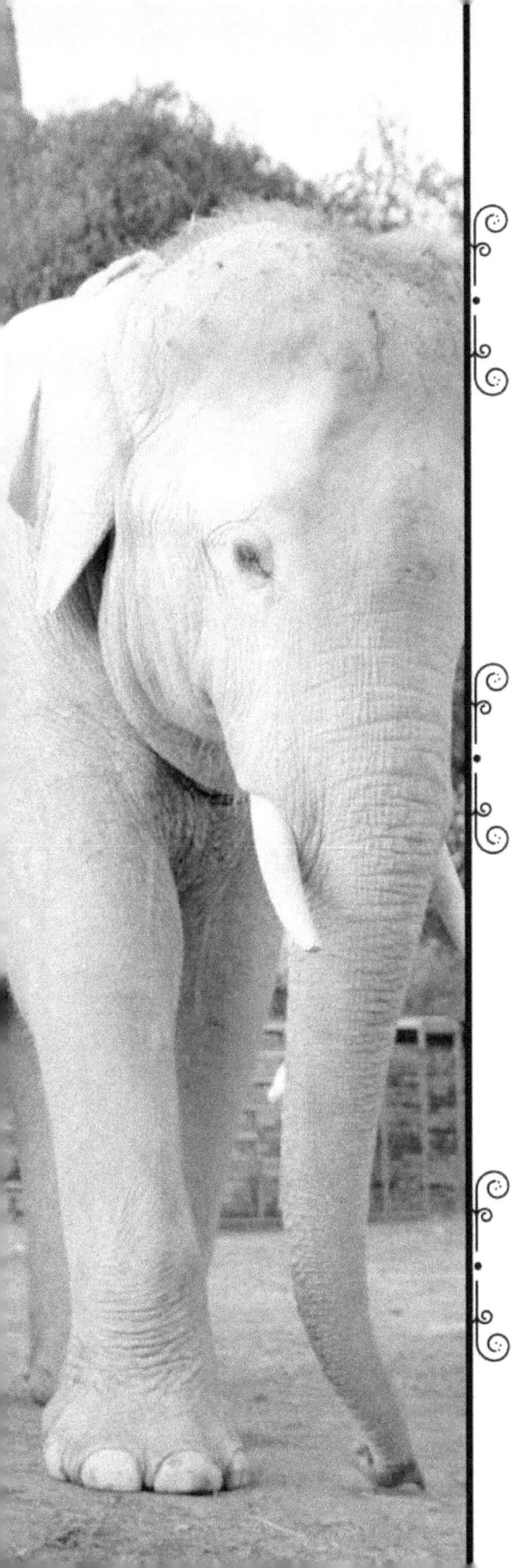

Don't expect others to promote your dream when they are struggling with their own reality.

Embrace life's
ups and downs
for when you
flat-line it's
all over.

Everyone lives
or has lived in a
glass house;
there should be
no stone-
throwing.

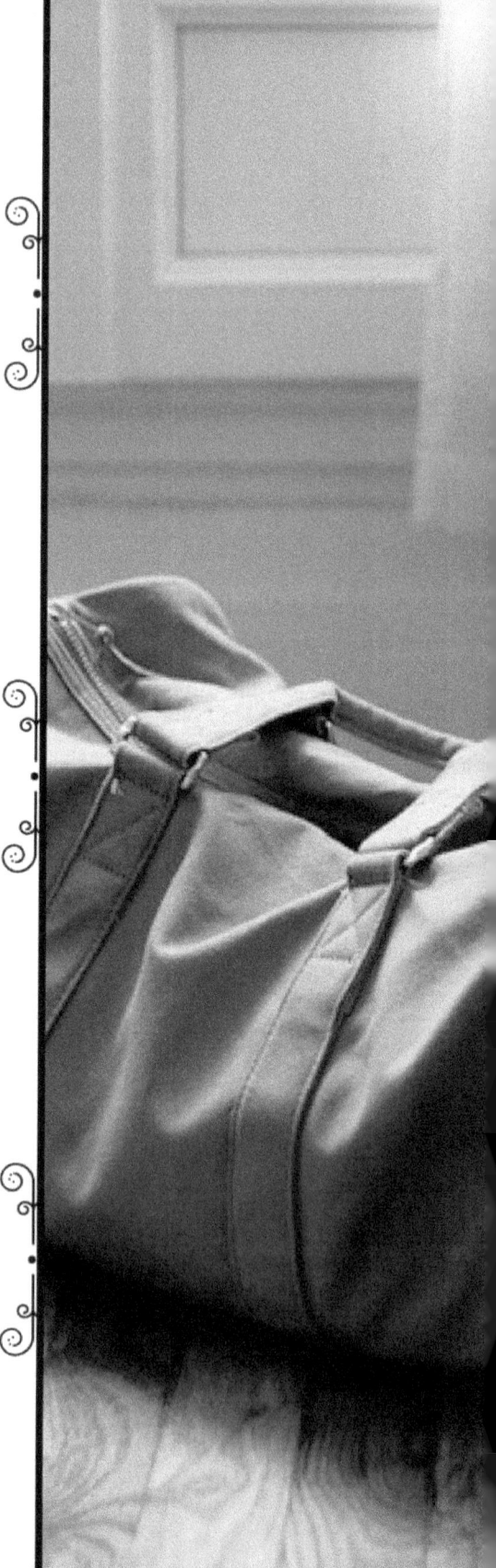

Everything comes
to an end at some
point – friendships
& relationships
included;
don't be afraid
to drop excess
baggage.

Fish can't throw his gorilla friend into the sea and expect him to swim.

Gratitude enriches
your attitude
improves your
aptitude
and heightens
your altitude;
focus on gratitude.

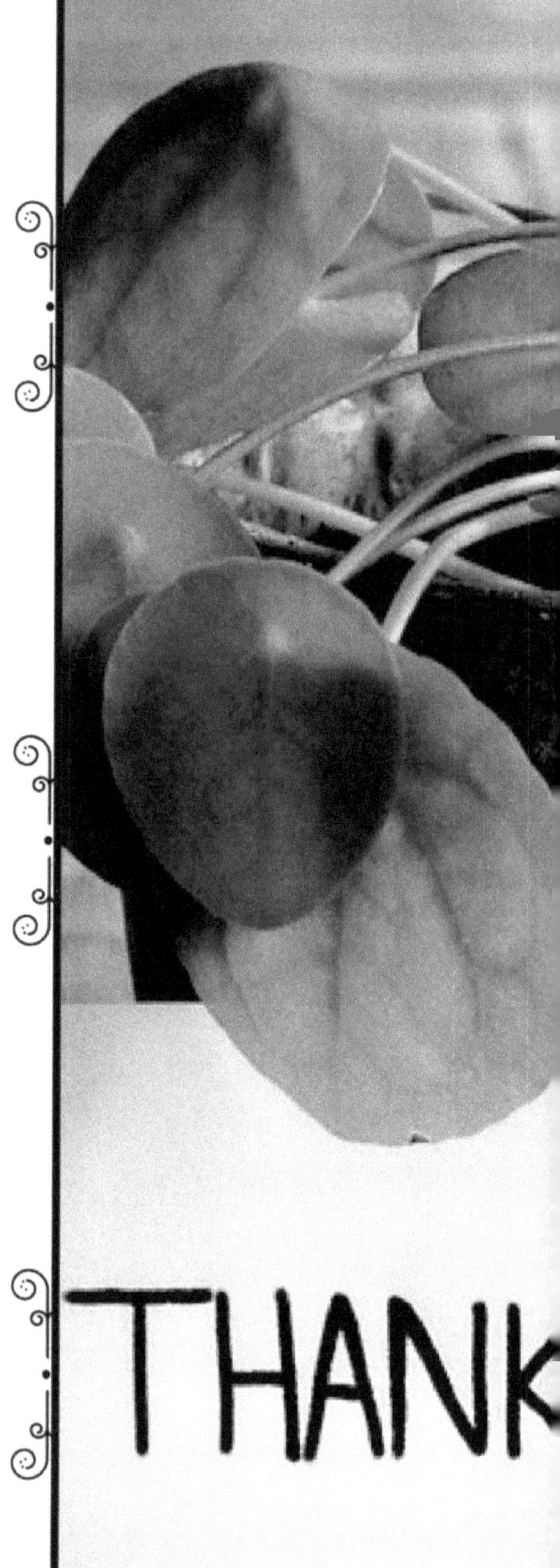

THANK

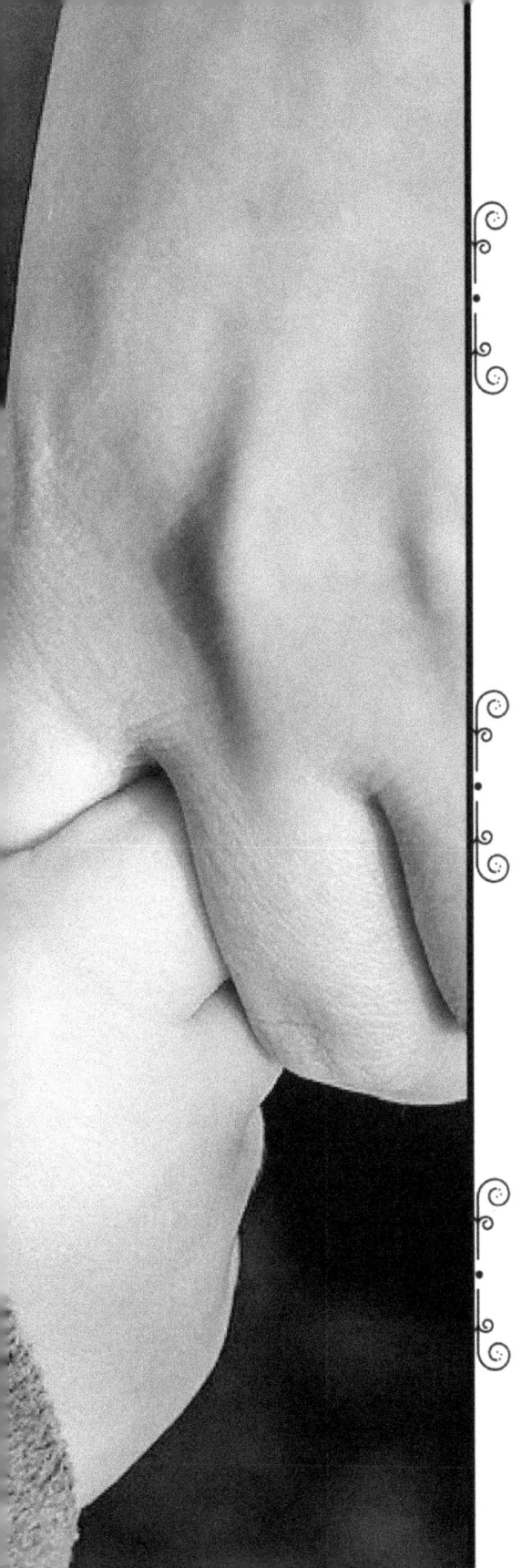

Giving and
receiving
are two sides of
the same coin;
you can't do one
without the
other.

He who shouts
the loudest
doesn't
necessarily have
all the facts.

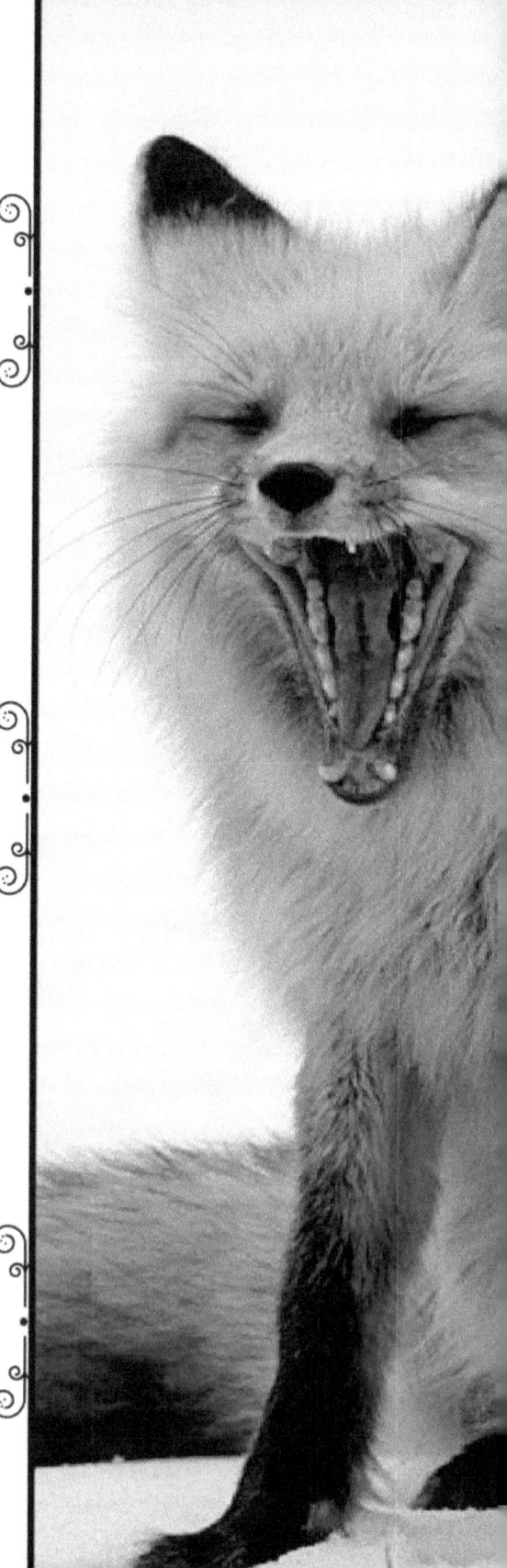

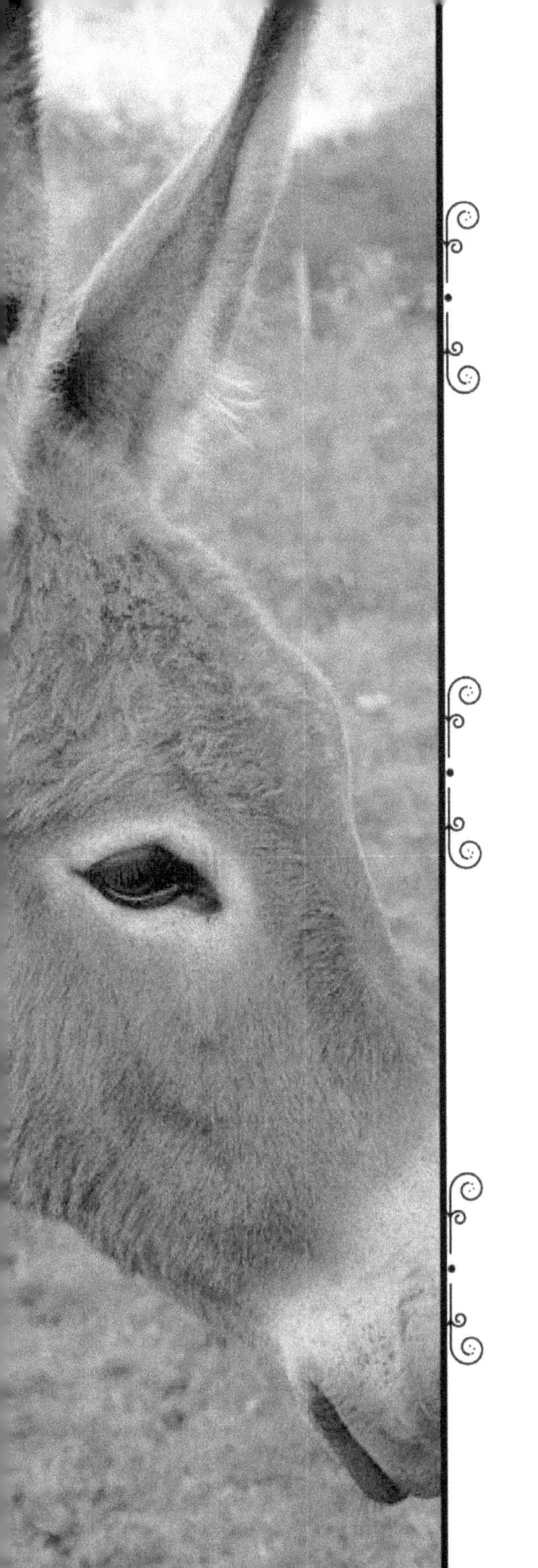

If you choose to
discuss
philosophy
with a donkey
you're an ass.

If you compare yourself with ants you'll worry about anthills.

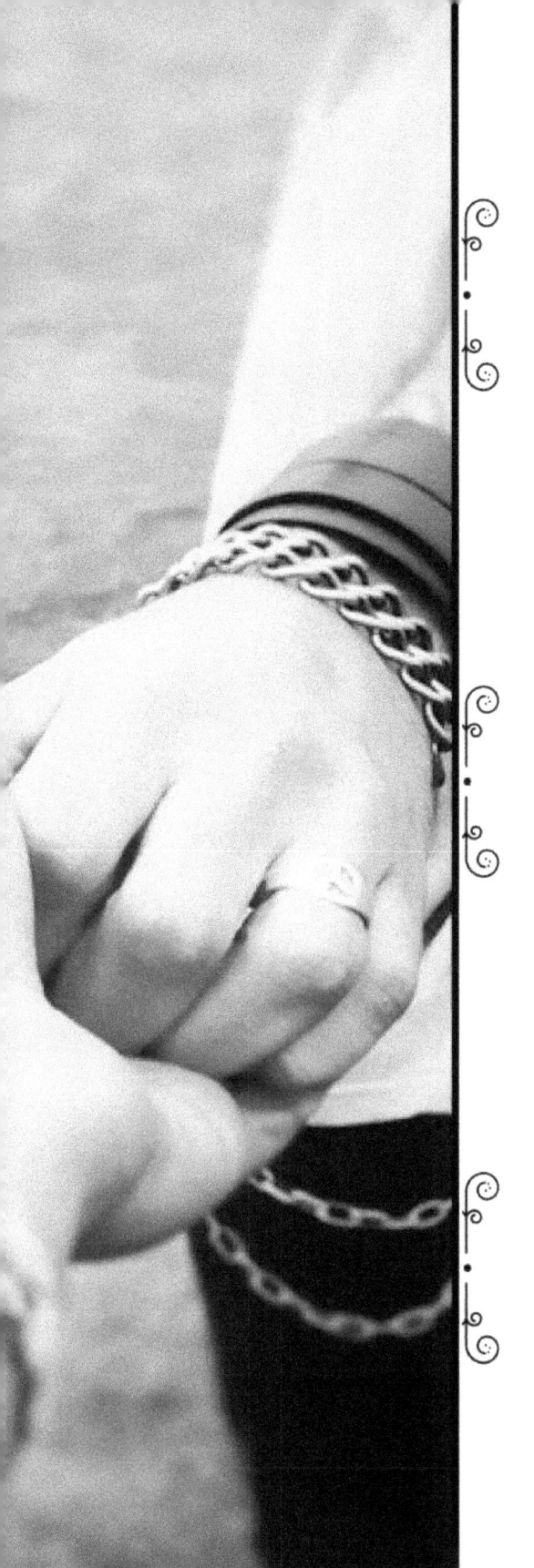

If you
consistently
try to pull up
someone who
insists on being a
dead weight
they'll eventually
pull you down.

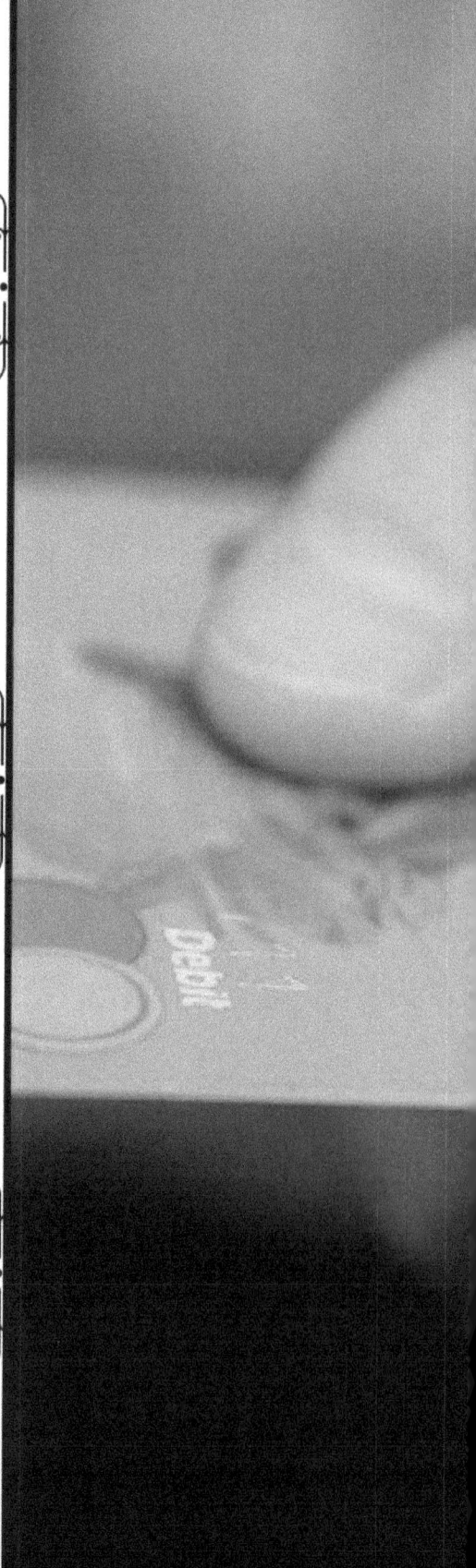

If you don't pay the price you won't appreciate the value.

If you're not
prepared to give
up something you
shouldn't expect
to take down
anything.

If you don't till
your soil
it will give rise
to weeds.

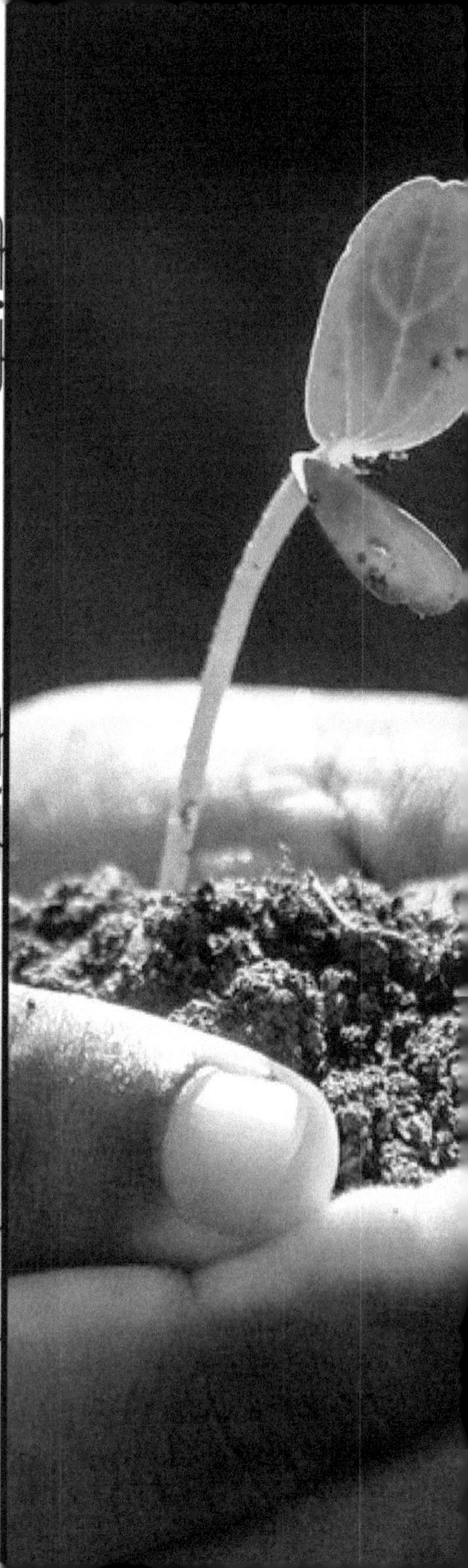

If you don't drive
you'll be driven;
one way or
another
you've got to
move!

If you don't see
what you need
on the outside,
go back and look
on the inside.

If you follow a bat you'll end up in a cave but you could learn to fly.

If you habitually consume rubbish you shouldn't be surprised if you start to gag.

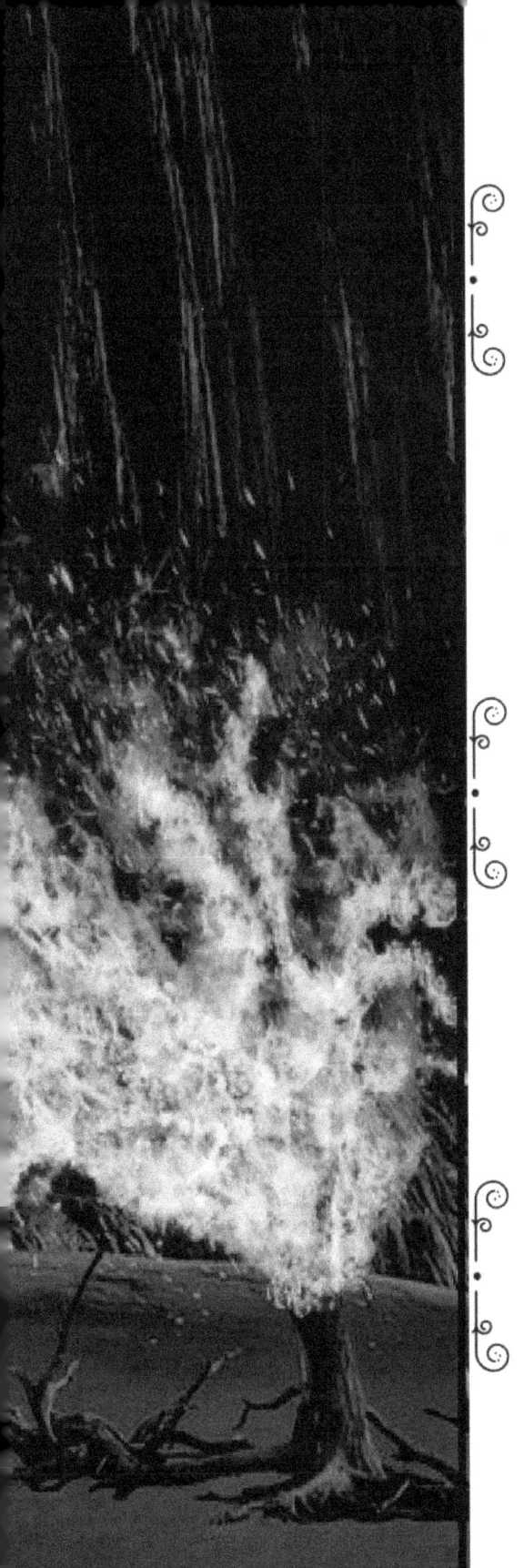

If you light a spark in a hot place it will ignite.

If you live on
the edge don't
be surprised if
you fall off.

If you surround yourself with losers you can't expect to win.

If you want
something
you've got to
go and get it;
it will not come
and get you.

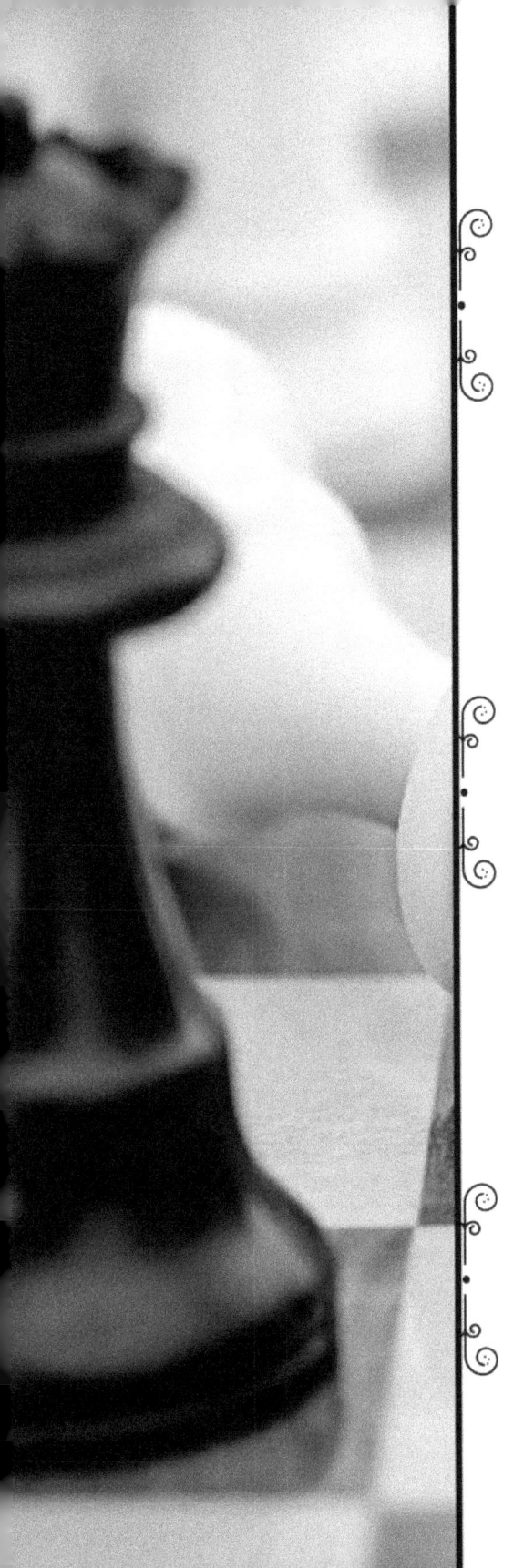

There's no point
watching from the
side-lines;
stay in the game,
even if you're
losing!

In the darkness
you can't perceive
of the light;
then the light
appears and
suddenly, the
darkness has
purpose.

It is better to run with winners and lose than to run with losers and win.

It's better to be the slowest eagle than the speediest chicken.

It's better to
say NO and feel
bad about it
than to say YES
and regret it.

It's impossible
to find your way
if you don't
know where
you're going.

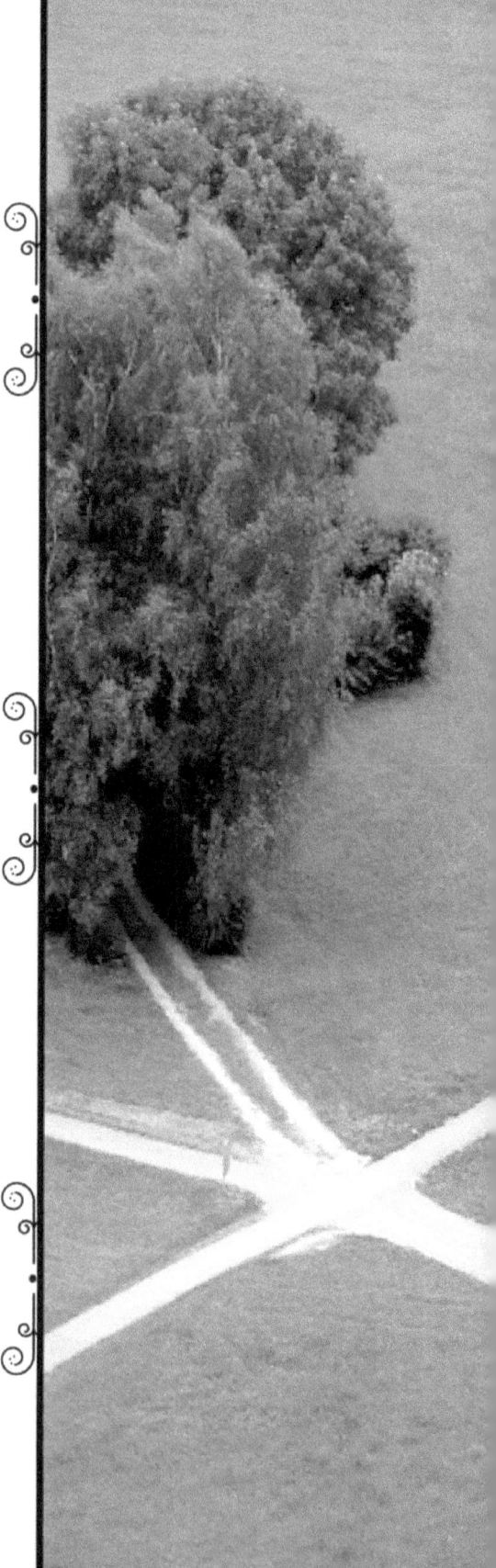

It's okay to use
somebody else'
ladder to get
where you want
to go;
just be grateful!

Life doesn't give
to one roses and
to the other
thorns;
we all have a
share of both.

Look behind you
and reach out;
the hand you take
may be your very
own.

"Movement" and
"Progress"
are not
synonymous.

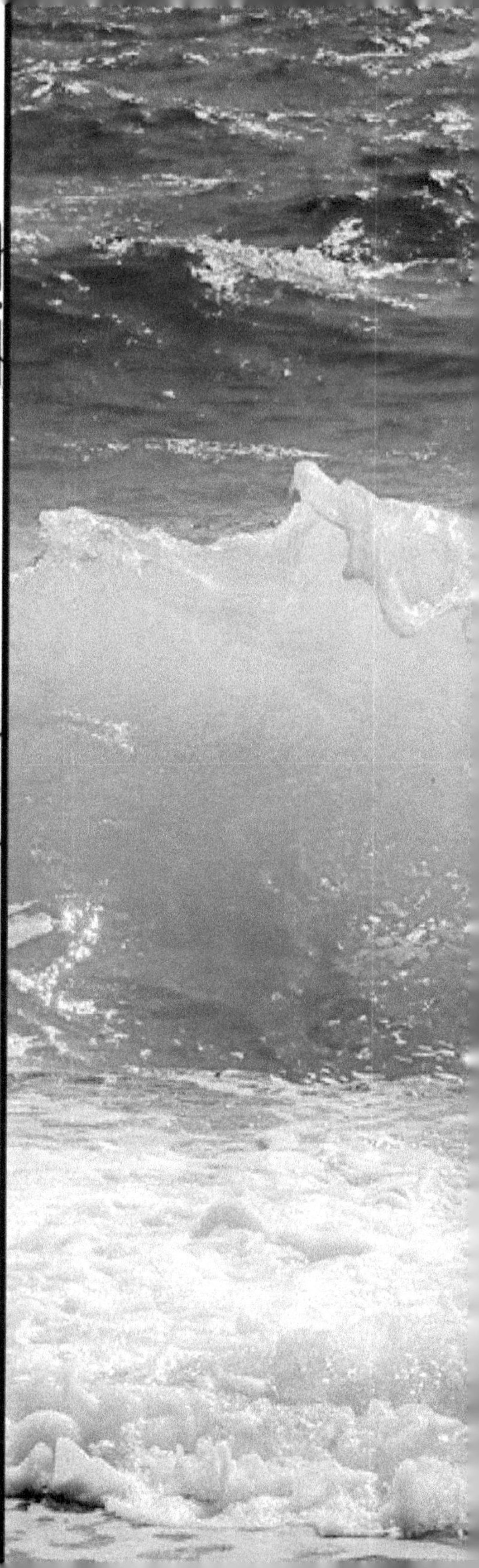

No one can help you water your garden if they don't know it exists.

No matter
how vast the
darkness,
the tiniest of
lights can
penetrate it.

No-one has to fall for you to rise.

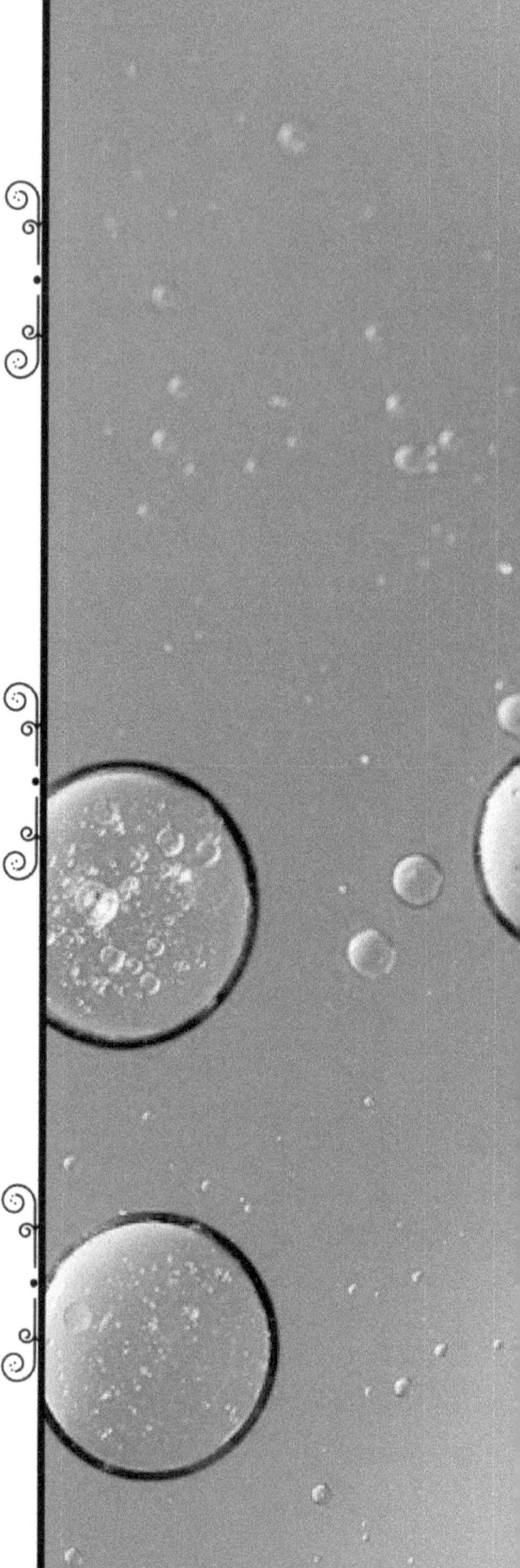

Oil and water may appear to mix but when the shaking is over they each settle into their natural state.

One day we
come to realise
what's truly
important in life
it's not money,
the job or stuff;
it's people!

One turn of the Ferris wheel is worth thousands of turns of the hamster wheel; faster isn't always better.

Open doors often
look like closed
doors;
move forward
and turn the
handle.

Opportunity
knocks
and not just
once.

Some lessons
are expensive;
get over it!

Some people are just not ready and you have to concede that you can't take them with you.

Sometimes we
have to meet
people just
where they are;
don't impose,
don't suppose,
don't transpose.

Sometimes we need people around who are going somewhere and who are willing to take us with them.

Sometimes your dream is wrapped up in somebody else' vision; keep an open mind.

That you got off
doesn't mean
you got away.

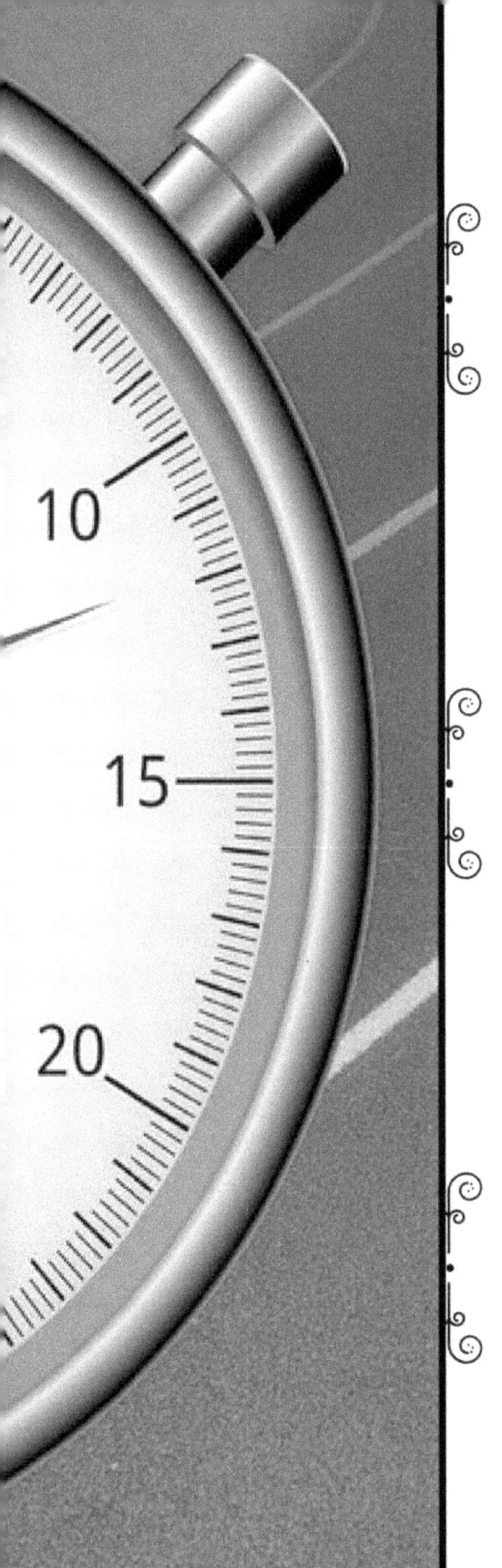

That you won a
10,000 m race
does not mean
you'll win a
100 m race.

The fact that
You can fit doesn't
mean
you will fit in;
choose your
space carefully.

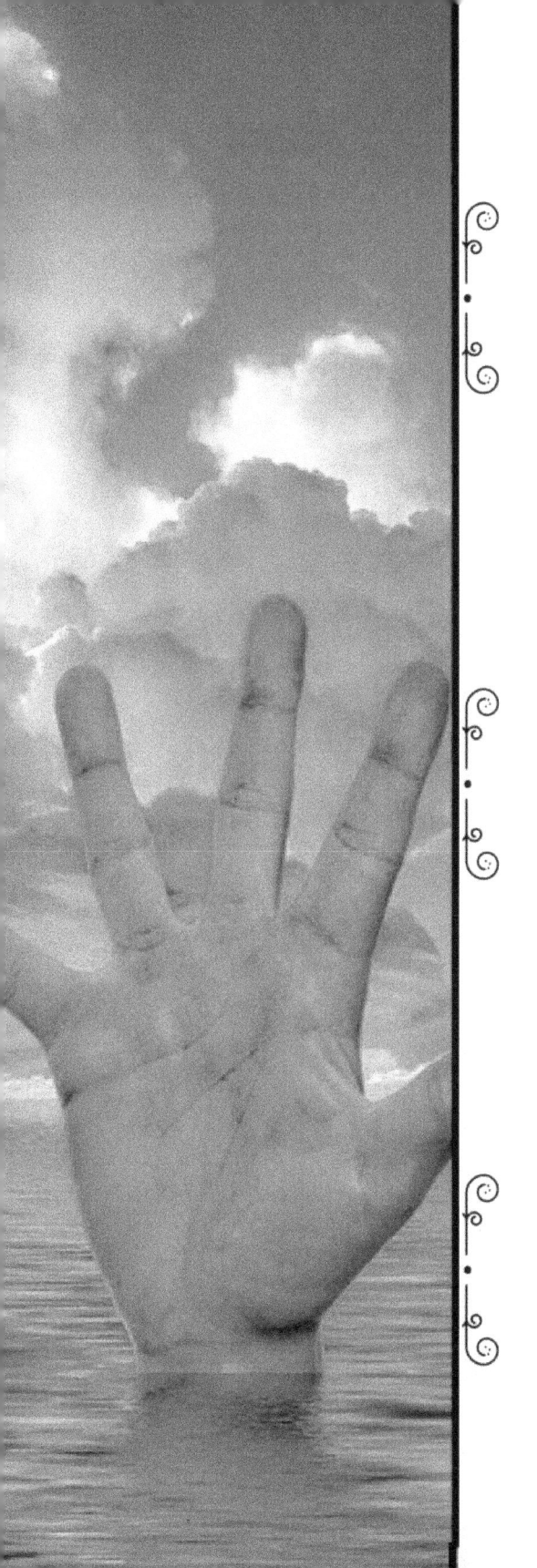

The fact that
you can swim
doesn't preclude
you from
drowning.

The flapping
comes before the
soaring;
get the sequence
wrong and
promptly comes
the falling.

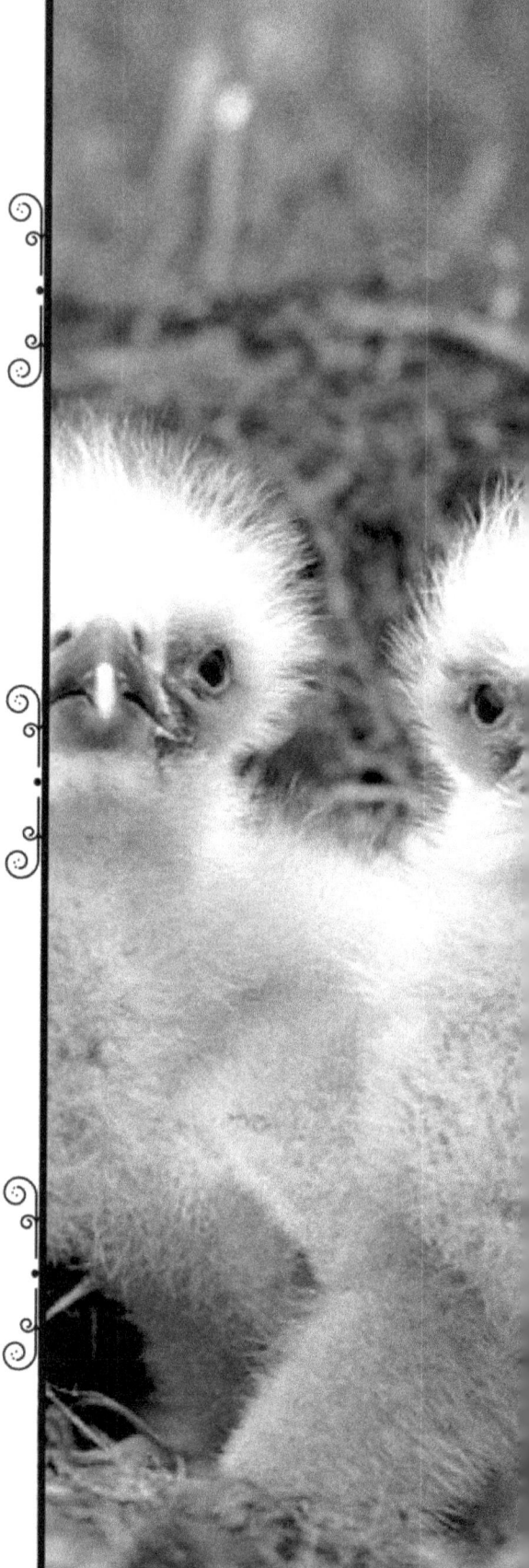

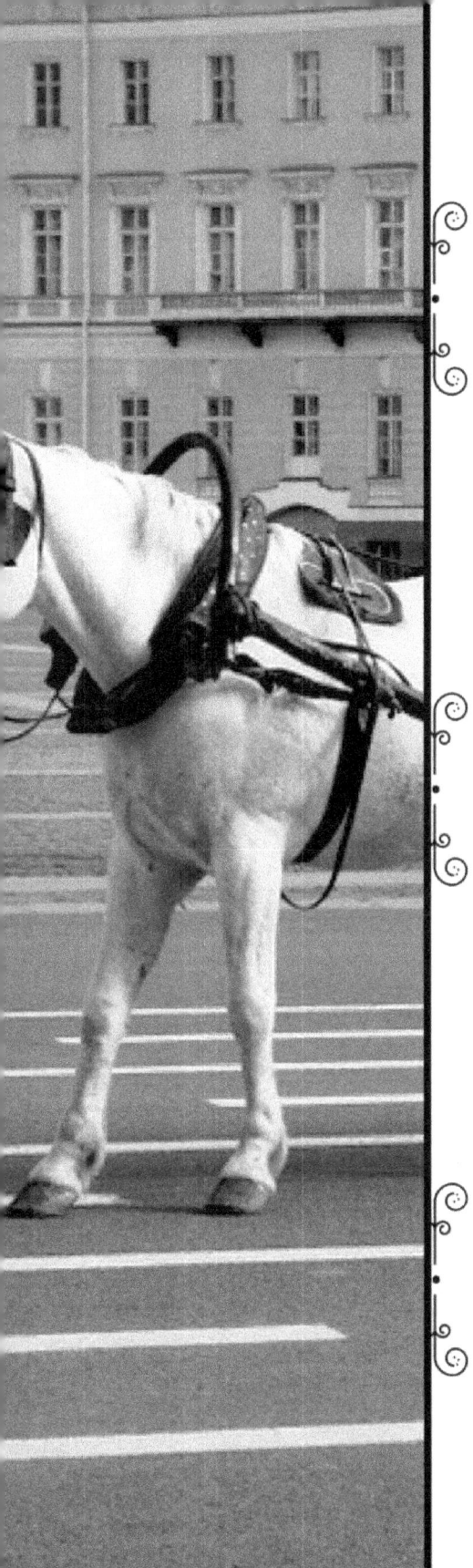

The only place where cart appears before horse is in the dictionary.

There's no point
presenting a gift
to someone
if they are not
in a space to
receive it.

There's nothing noble in refusing to quit if you're consistently the weak link.

Those who don't understand the issues on the ground will doggedly promote their pie in the sky.

TIME is the
master,
a healer and
great revealer.

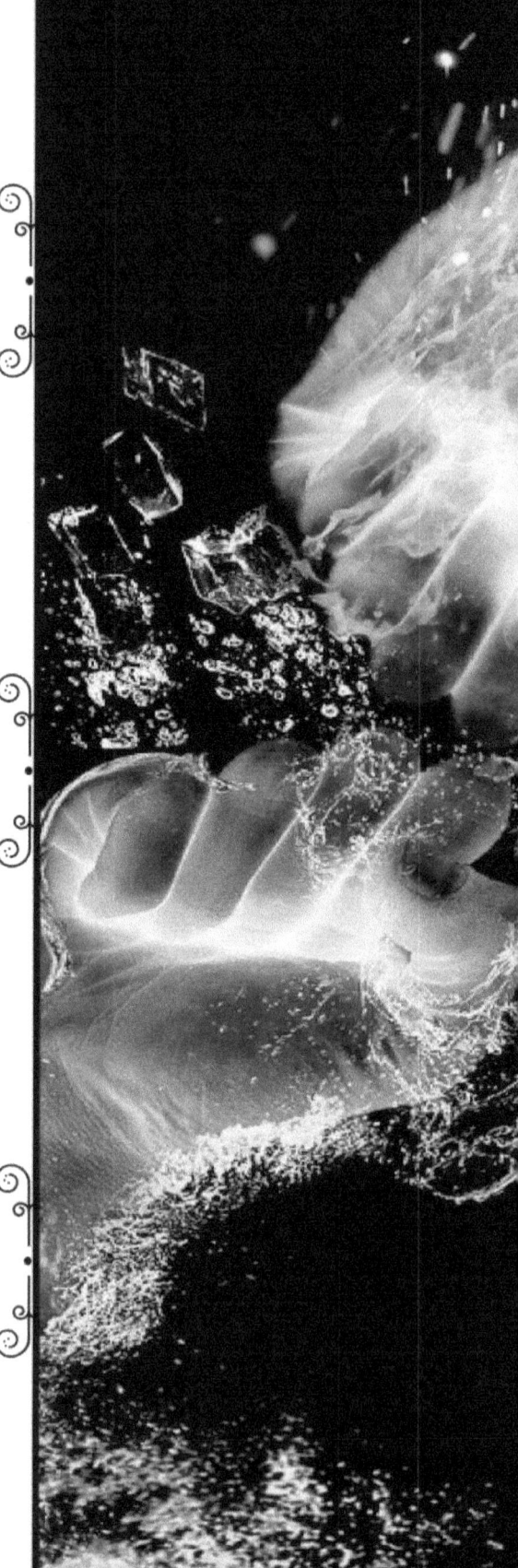

Too much of a
good thing is not a
good thing.
You need water
but too much
water will
drown you;
you need fire
but too much fire
will burn you.

Treasures don't
float;
you've got to dig
and dive.

Success is not measured in numbers; ultimately each must determine his own currency.

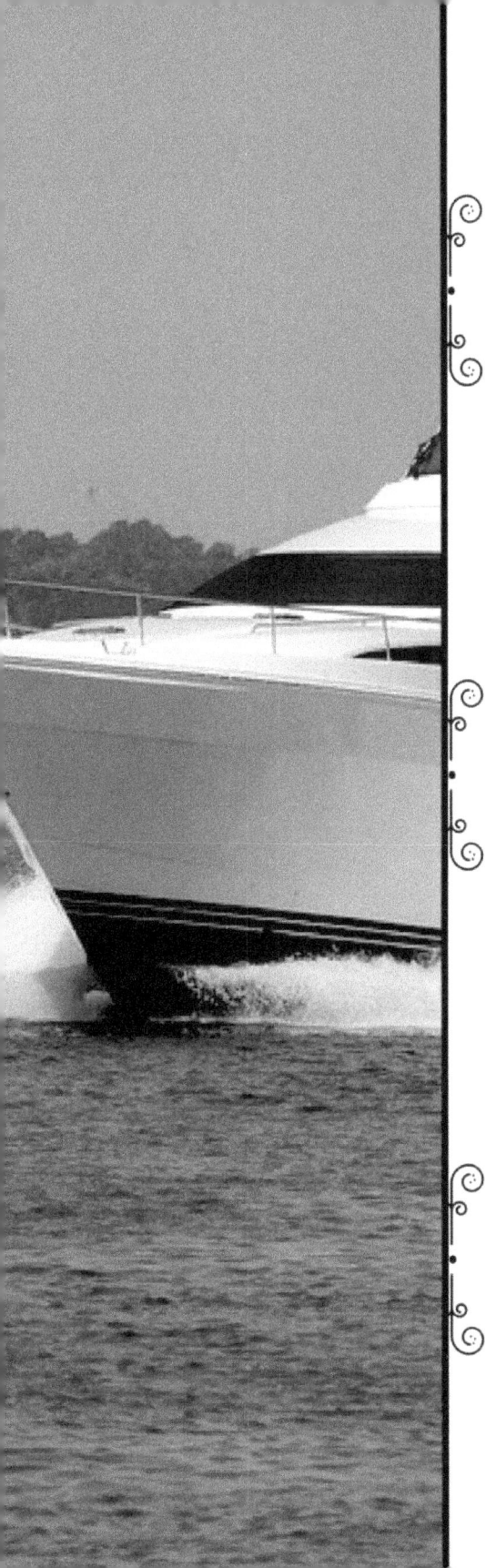

We are poor
together but
wealthy apart.

We must learn
to recognise
when someone's
part in our story
is over;
thank them and
let them go!

When I propel
someone forward
I move forward
too.

You can't curse
Caesar in his
Palace.

You can't hop on
to another
person's boat
and claim it
as your own;
unless you're a
pirate!

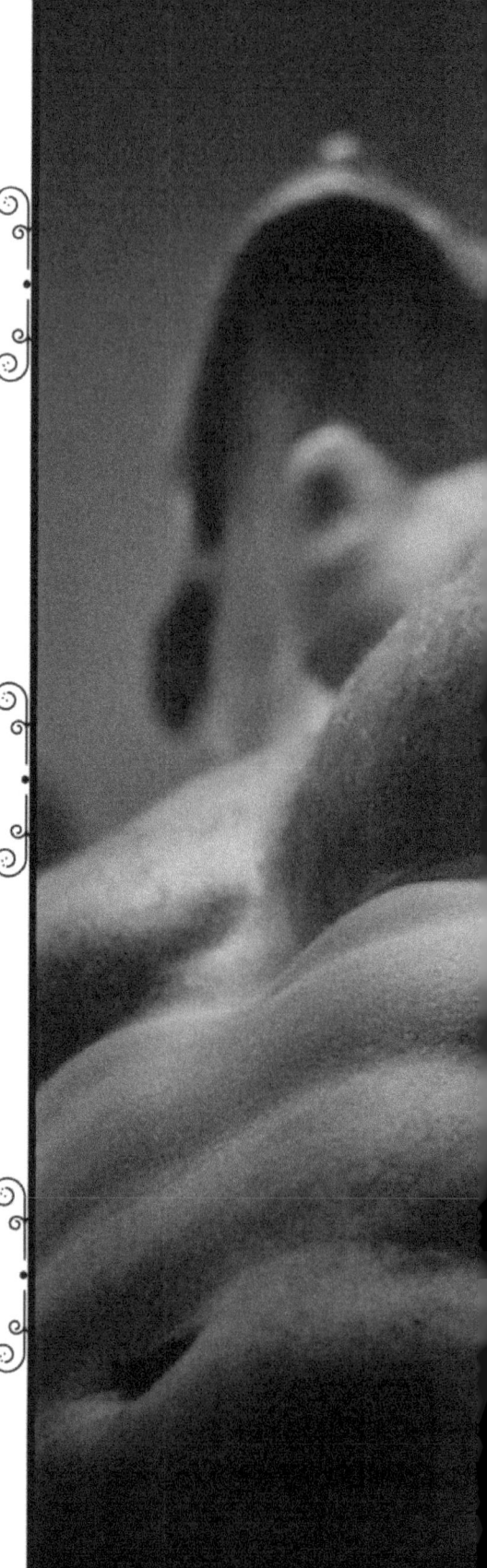

You don't have
to flex your
muscles in order
to win;
learn to drop it,
leave it and
let it go.

You don't need
to grow in order
to reach;
you need to reach
in order to grow.

You just cannot share the light with people who insist on keeping their eyes closed.

You may be able to achieve anything but there is a season for everything and at some point that season passes.

Your circumstances
don't define you;
they refine you.

Your dream is
planted inside
of you;
don't worry if
others can't see it
or don't share it;
just don't let
them stifle it.

Your mentor is
not the person
who advises you;
it's the one
whose advice
you follow.

PART 2

LOVE

Love is patient, love is
kind.
It does not envy,
it does not boast,
it is not proud.
It does not dishonor
others,
it is not self-seeking,
it is not easily angered,
it keeps no record
of wrongs.
Love does not delight
in evil but rejoices
with the truth.
It always protects,
always trusts, always
hopes,
always perseveres.
Love never fails.

1 Corinthians 13: 4-8

An 8-year old
child dies,
an 80 year old
man dies;
it's the same thing
but it's not the
same.

Happiness starts
within.

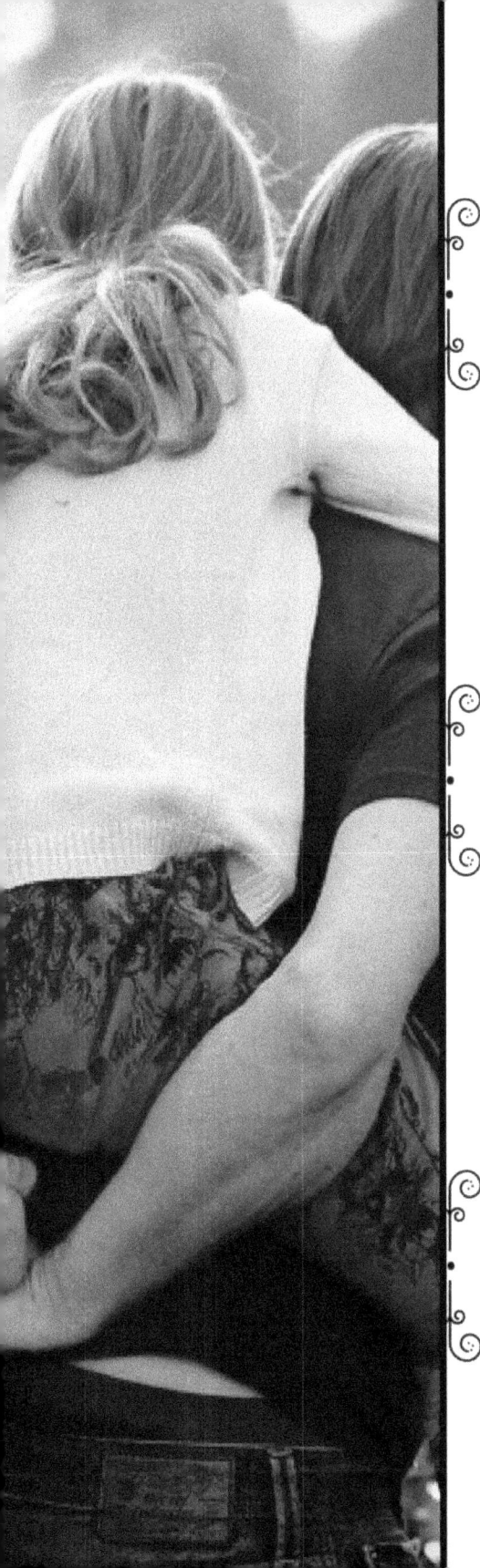

It's fine to carry the bride during the honeymoon but at some point she's expected to walk.

Love is like a
baton; it's made
for passing.

One may be a
whole number but
it takes
two to tango.

Your life is littered
with love and
hate;
love some things
and hate others.
Choose carefully.

PART 3

SPIRIT

The fruit of the Spirit is love, joy, peace, forbearance, kindness, goodness, faithfulness, gentleness and self-control.

Galatians 5: 22-23

God doesn't give
us furniture,
houses, paper
or pianos.
He gives us
trees!

God is not
impressed
by stupidity.

If you just look
at the soil you'll
never think
there's oil;
dig deep and
deeper still.

If you rip off people you won't get very far; and if you do, you'll have to turn around eventually!

Light is best
appreciated in
the presence of
darkness;
be grateful for
your darkest
days!

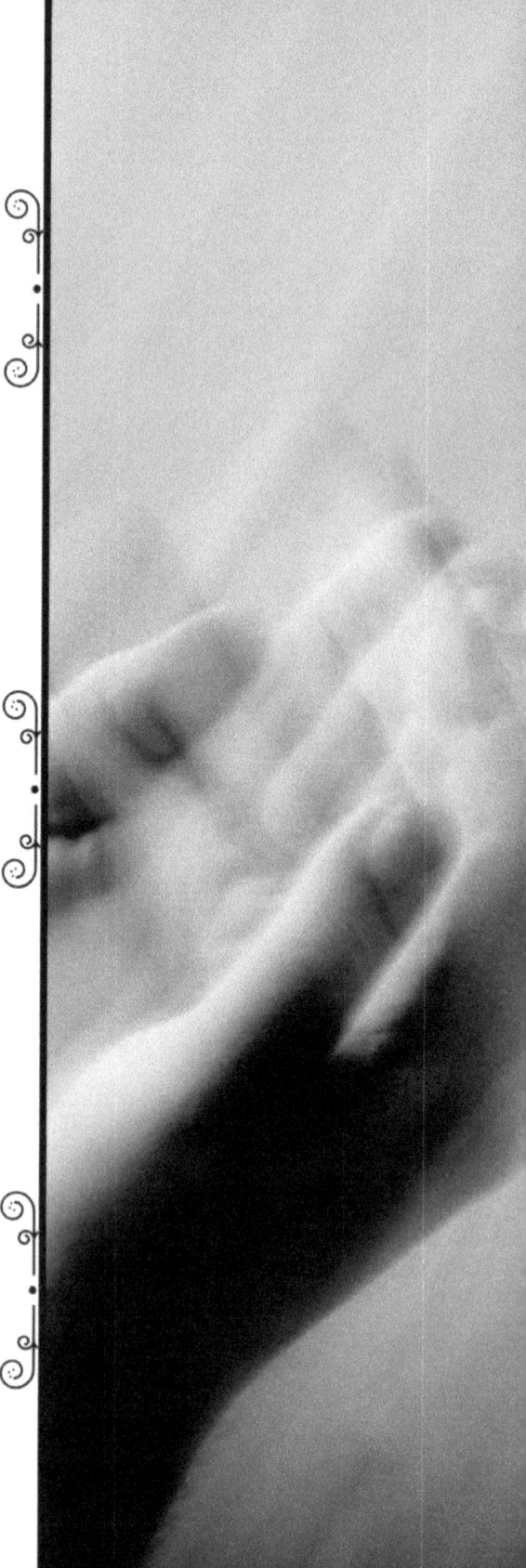

Many of us are
waiting on God;
when in fact God
is waiting on us.

Many of us talk
God
but don't do
God.

One person
sees a hole;
another sees an
opening.

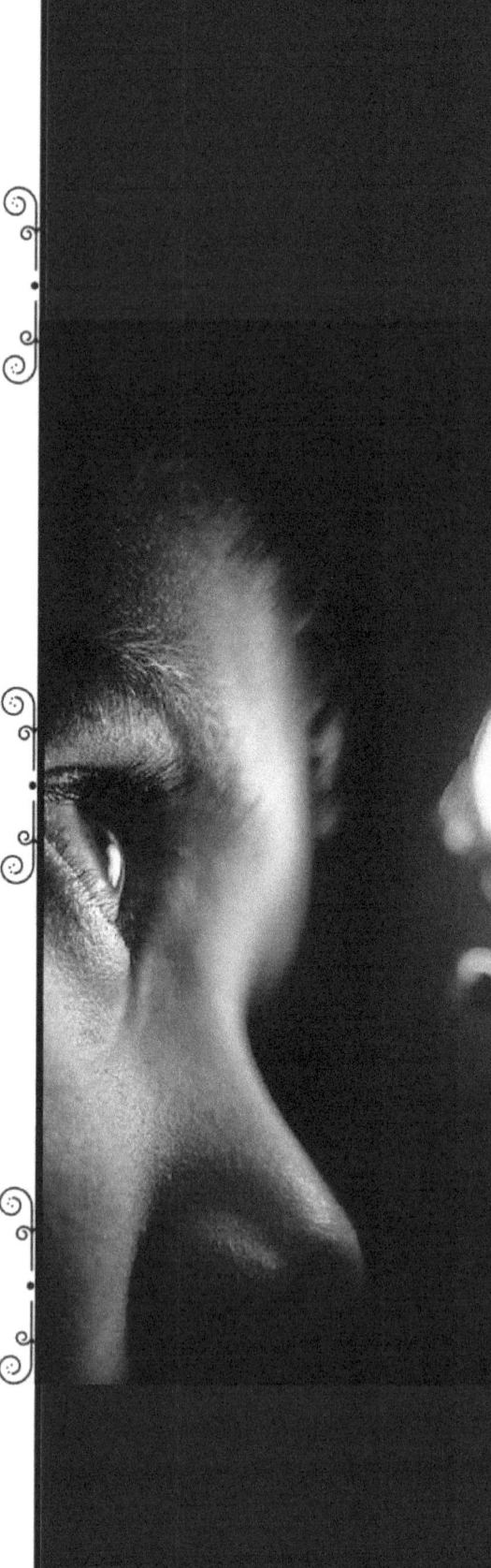

Our knees and our
feet share
The same limb;
prayer without
action goes
nowhere.

Rise and Fall,
Up and Down,
Success and
Failure are all
twins;
remember this in
your interactions
with people.

See those
obstacles along
the way;
not in your way.

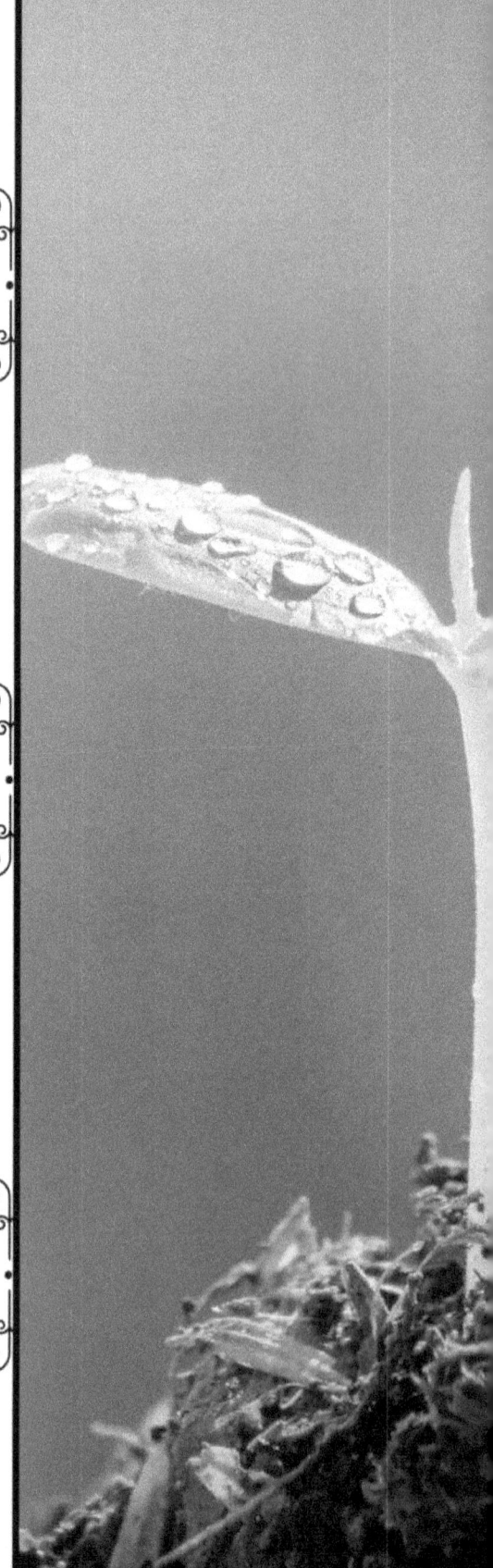

Seed is more
powerful than
fruit.

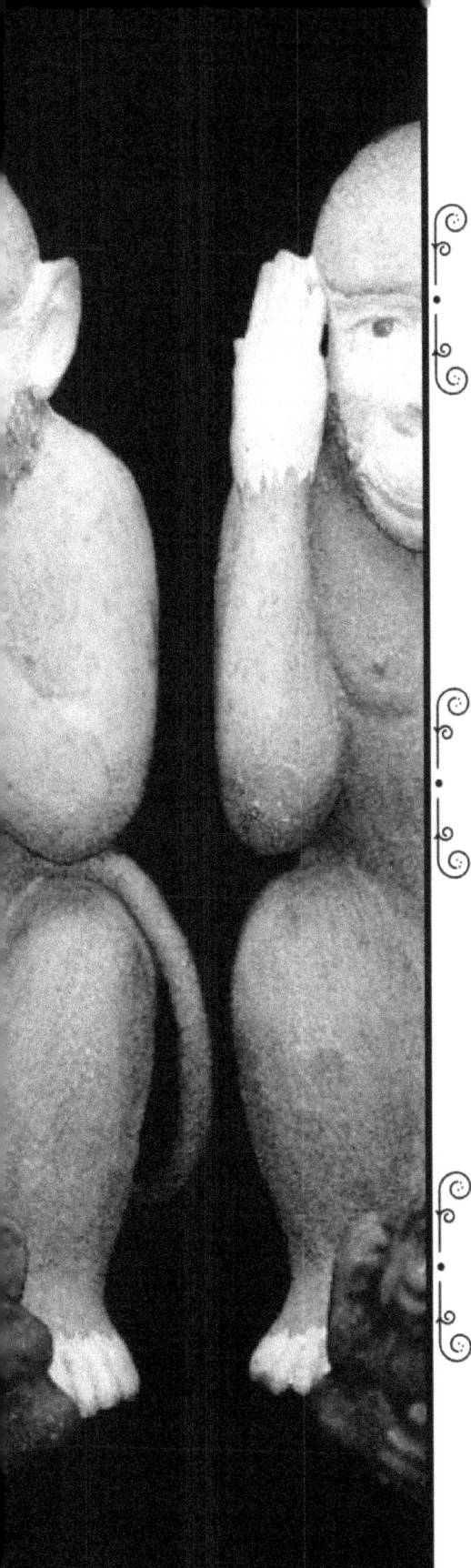

Silence
is not golden
where injustice
reigns.

Some things are
better wiped
than washed.

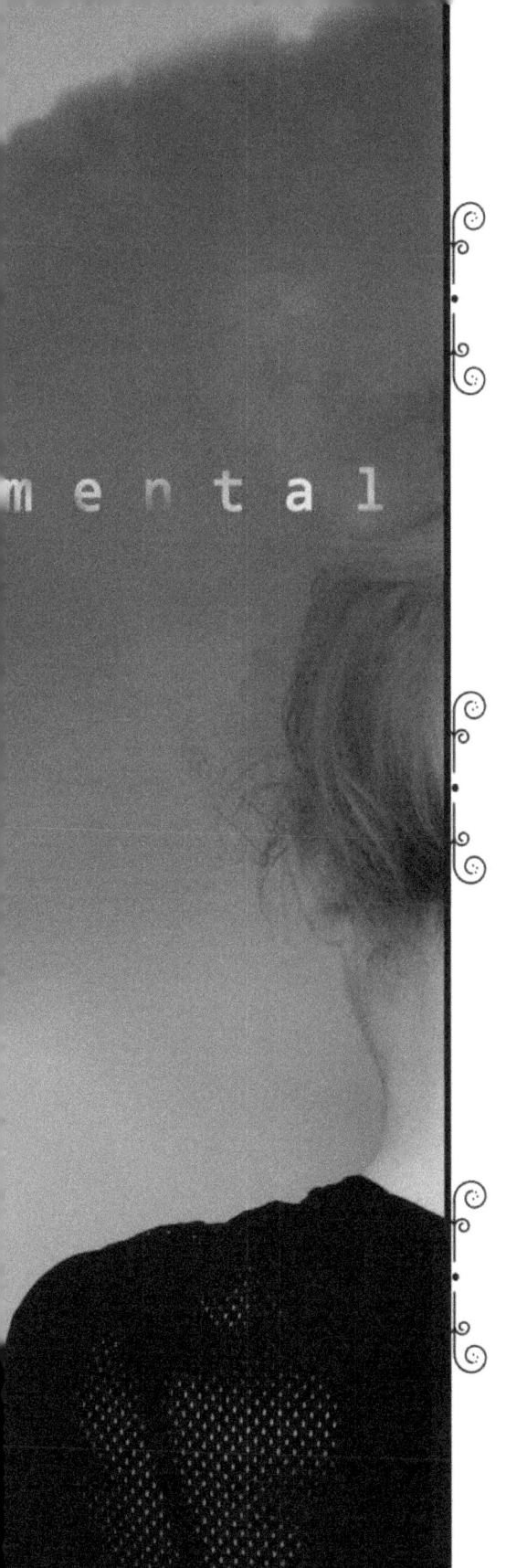

m e n t a l

To avoid
breakdown:
Break in, break off,
break up,
break out and
Breakthrough!

Trees bear fruit,
fruits have seeds,
seeds hold trees;
everyone, indeed
everything has
something to offer
in the cycle of life.

True joy is in
the giving,
not in the
getting.

We can dress up as much as we want, people are only interested in our spirit; for once it leaves they get rid of our body.

We can say
anything
we want to say
but our actions
will always reveal
the truth.

We can tell
people what
we want them
to believe;
but we have to
live with our
own truth.

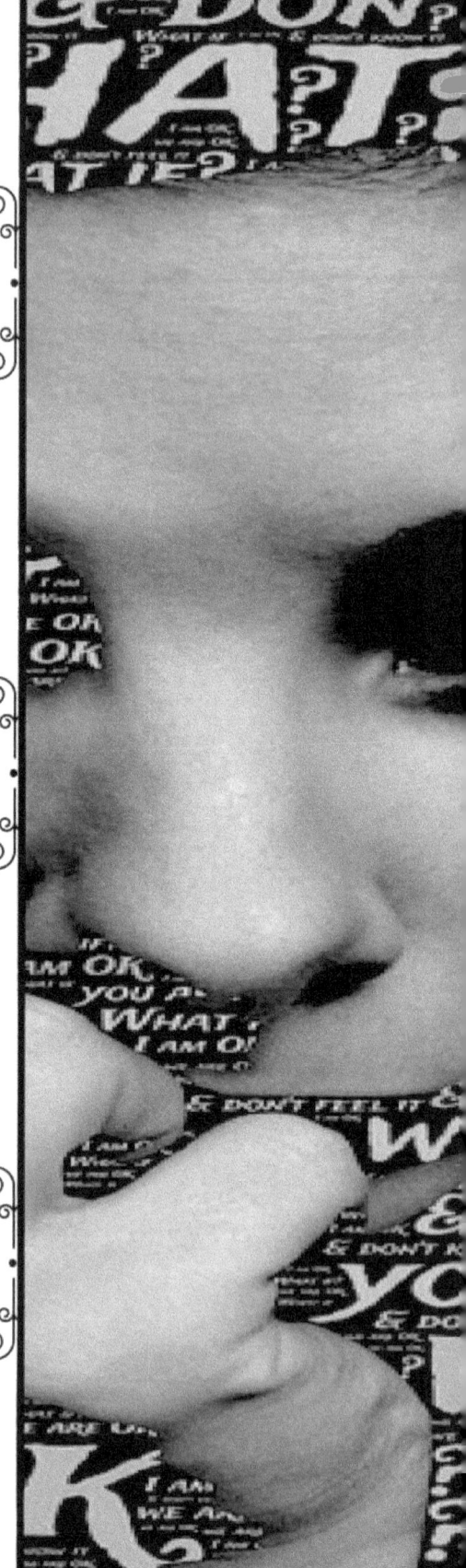

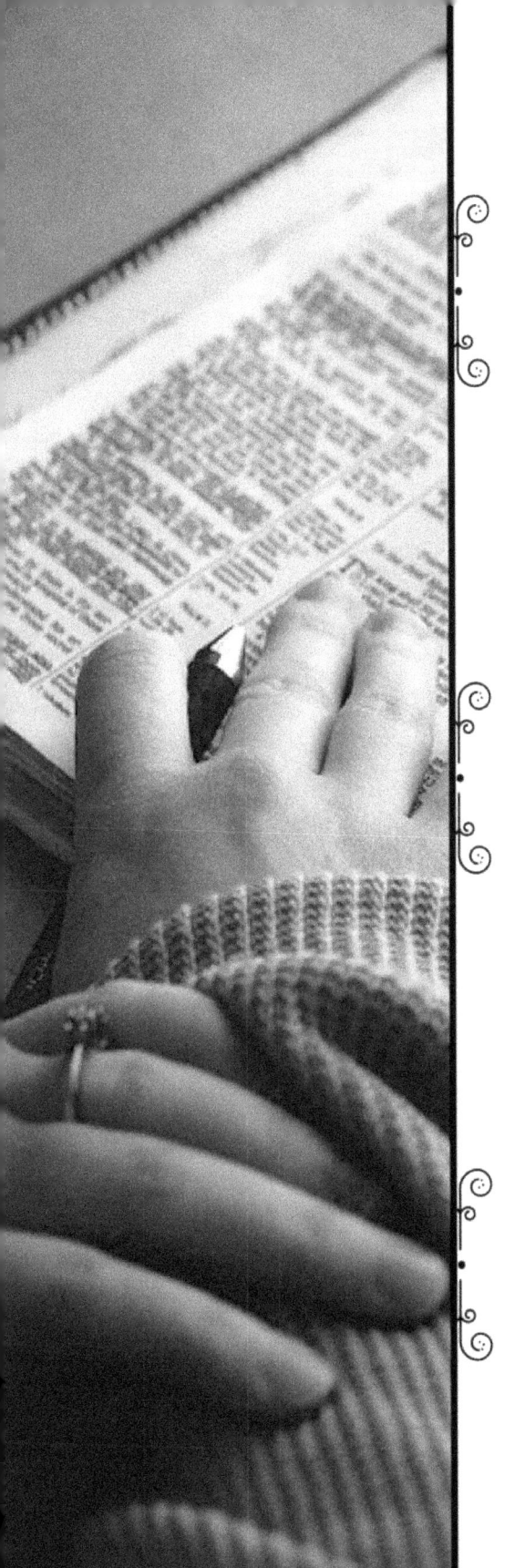

We can't speak
and things
happen;
only God can
do that.

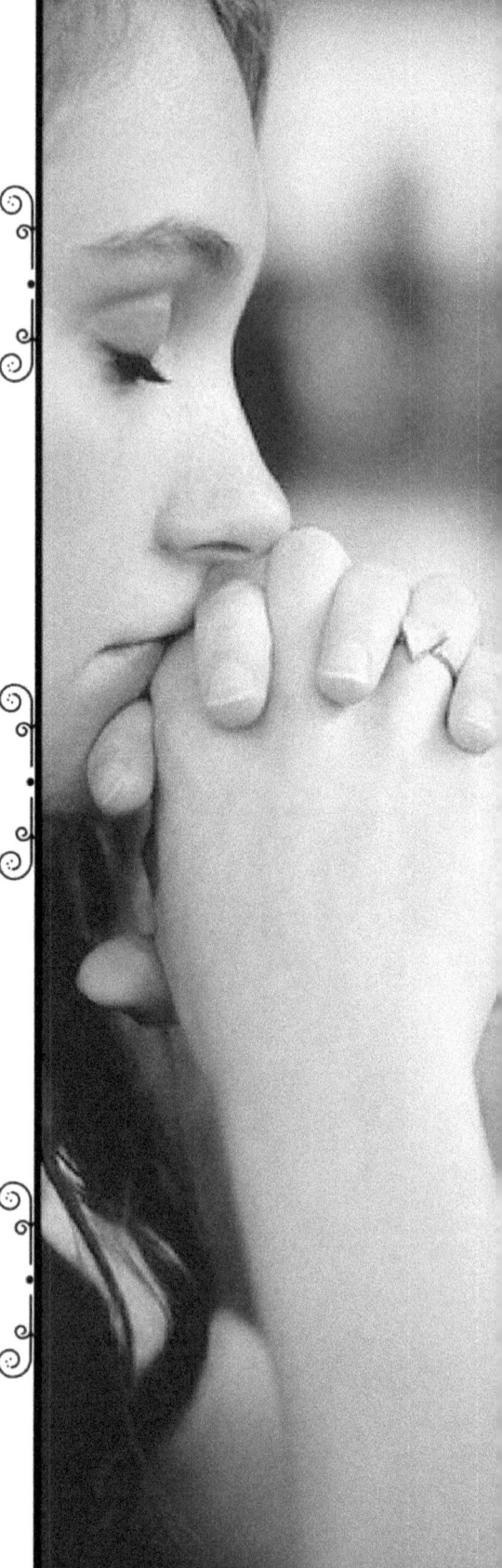

We have no right
to ask for more
if we haven't
used what we've
been given.

We spend a great
deal of time
chasing money;
but if money is
all we have we
are poor indeed.

We're forced to react to the world outside but we actively respond to the world we've created on the inside.

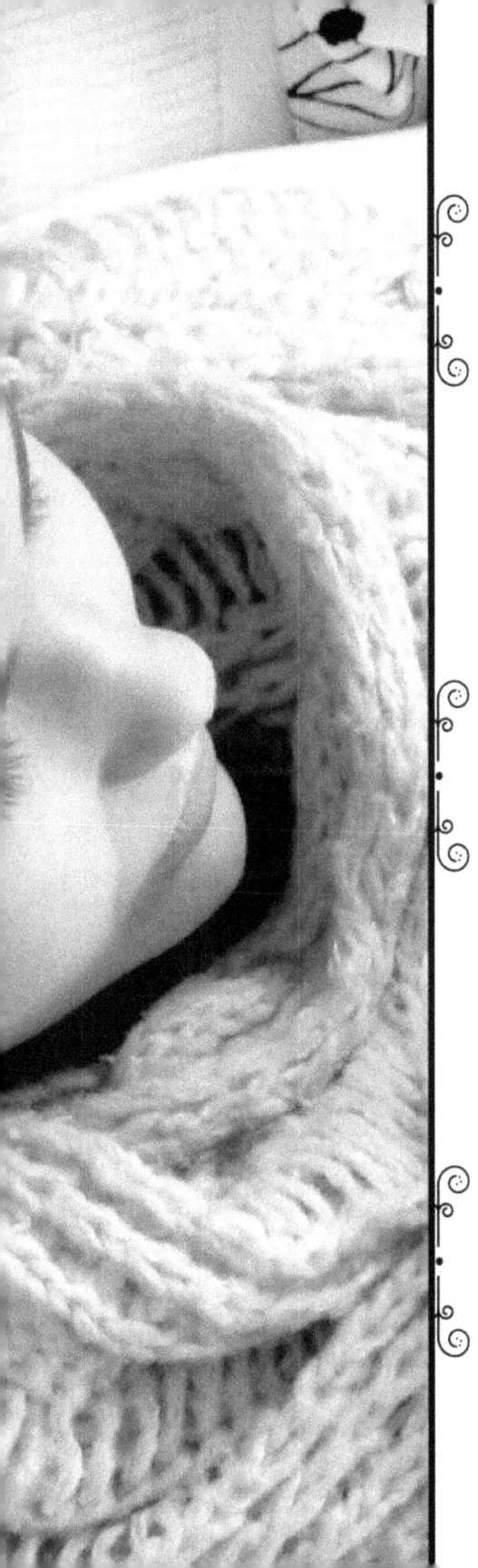

Whatever pain
you encounter
in life learn to
get over it
for if you don't,
it will get over
you.

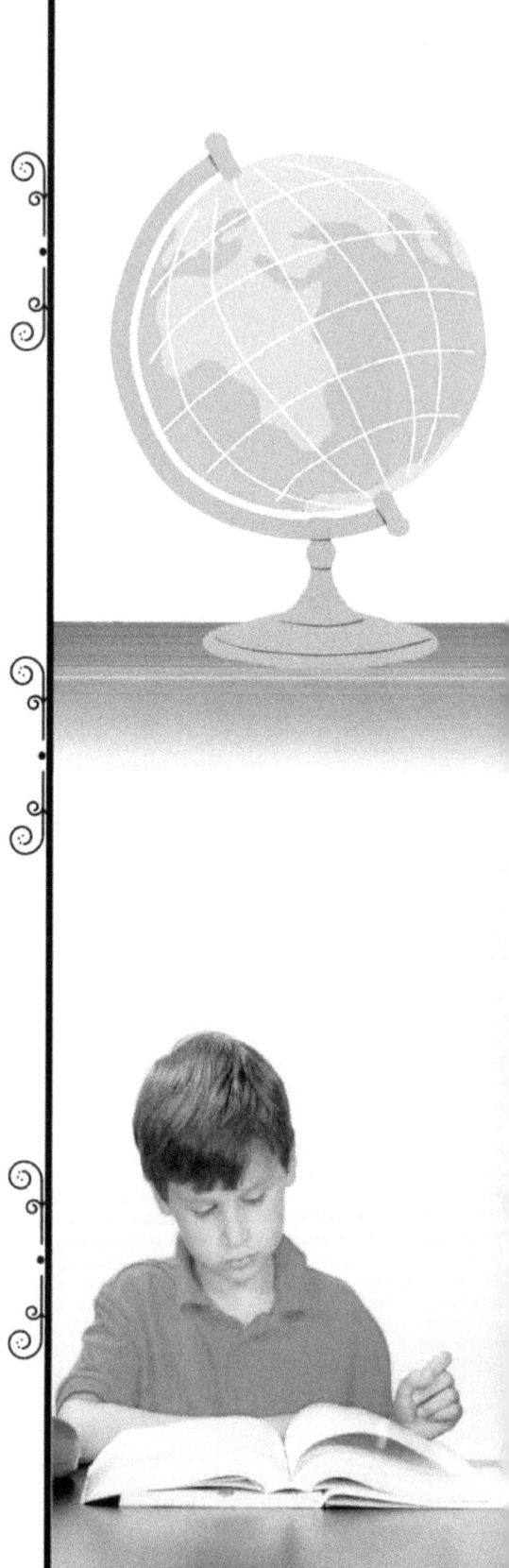

Whatever we
receive from the
outside cannot
compare with
what we have
on the inside.

You can never
soar like an eagle
if you sustain the
mind of a chicken.

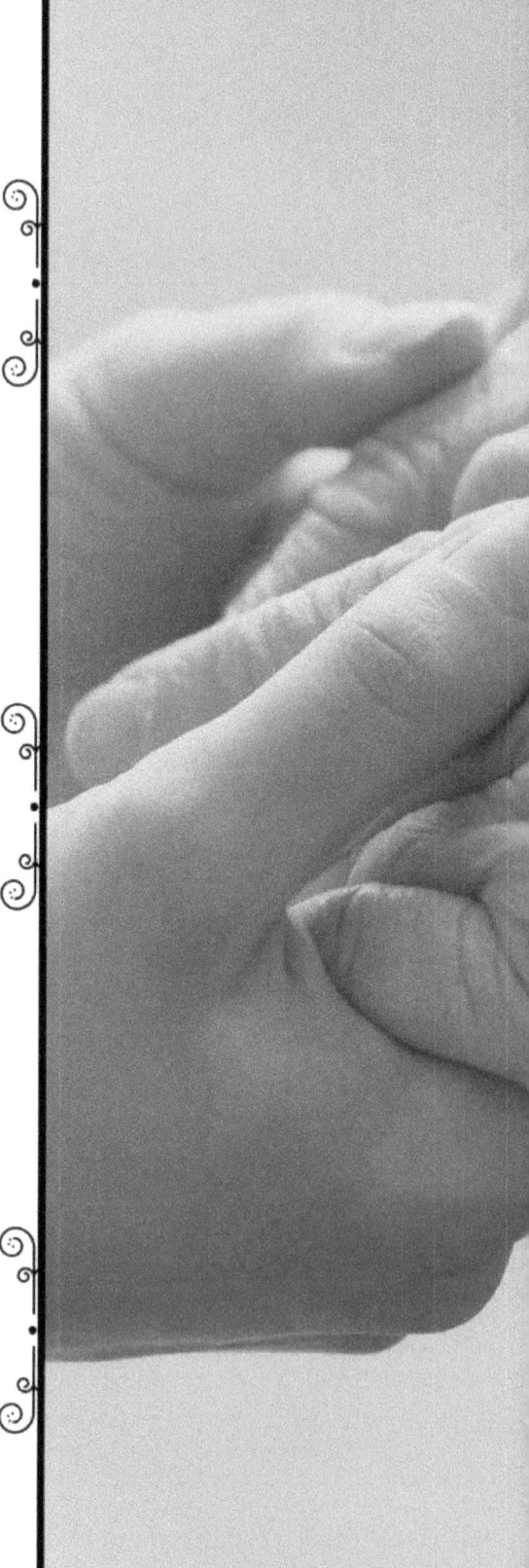

You can't be all things to all men but you can be one thing to one man.

You can't be a
servant of God
if you are busy
making yourself
a god to servants.

You don't need
a miracle
to be a miracle
to someone.

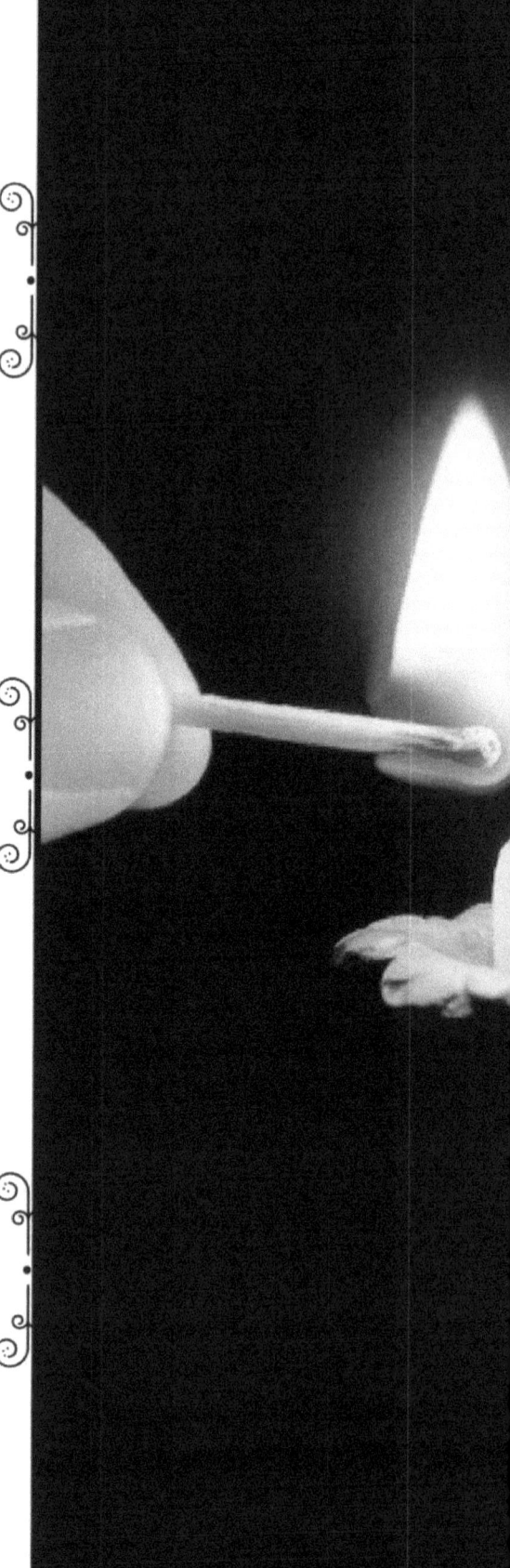

Another Book You'll Love

Life Lessons from a Bouncing Ball

https://amzn.to/3AUCH06

 This book is a much-needed reminder that play is not just for kids. Apart from stimulating joy and enhancing relaxation, play boosts our creativity and imagination and positively impacts our relationships and personal success.

Researchers have found that play isn't just about having fun; it can also be an important means of reducing stress and enhancing our overall well-being.

Please Leave a Review

I hope you enjoyed this text. Reviews are important to me as an independent author with a small marketing budget. So please remember to leave a review if you bought this book online.

Also, please note that if you purchased the text in a physical store or received the book as a gift, you can still leave a review on Amazon.

Thank you for acquiring this book, and thanks on behalf of the families who will benefit from your support.

ABOUT THE AUTHOR

Andrea Campbell, MBA, MA, is a social entrepreneur, linguist, and inspirational writer. Since publishing her first business book in 2010, Andrea has released several inspirational books and articles about special needs parenting and personal development, including two Amazon No. 1 bestsellers.

Over the years, she has focused on empowering vulnerable people through education and inspiration. As the mother of a child with special educational needs, she is particularly keen on working with families to enable their disabled children to aspire higher and achieve their potential. She also developed the Pocket Learner – a set of award-winning innovative educational resources for parents, caregivers and educators of children with special educational needs.

Andrea has also published various inspirational coloring books, journals, logs and activity books to empower and inspire people everywhere.

Andrea resides with her family in London, UK, where she continues to positively impact through her writing, creative exploits, training programs, coaching, philanthropy, and inspirational speaking.

Lightning Source UK Ltd.
Milton Keynes UK
UKHW022245301222
414639UK00002B/16